LIVING IN... SOUTH AFRICA

by Chloe Perkins
illustrated by Tom Woolley

READY-TO-READ

SIMON SPOTLIGHT

An imprint of Simon & Schuster Children's Publishing Division • New York   London   Toronto   Sydney   New Delhi • 1230 Avenue of the Americas, New York, New York 10020 • This Simon Spotlight edition October 2016 • Text copyright © 2016 by Simon & Schuster, Inc. Illustrations copyright © 2016 by Tom Woolley • All rights reserved, including the right of reproduction in whole or in part in any form. SIMON SPOTLIGHT, READY-TO-READ, and colophon are registered trademarks of Simon & Schuster, Inc. For information about special discounts for bulk purchases, please contact Simon & Schuster Special Sales at 1-866-506-1949 or business@simonandschuster.com. Manufactured in the United States of America 0916 LAK   2   4   6   8   10   9   7   5   3   1

Library of Congress Cataloging-in-Publication Data
Names: Perkins, Chloe, author. | Woolley, Tom, 1981- illustrator. Title: Living in . . . South Africa / by Chloe Perkins ; illustrated by Tom Woolley. Other titles: South Africa | Living in . . . (Simon and Schuster, Inc.) Description: New York : Simon & Schuster, 2016. | Series: Living in . . . | "Simon spotlight." Identifiers: LCCN 2016008603 | ISBN 9781481470926 (trade paper) | ISBN 9781481470933 (hardcover) | ISBN 9781481470940 (eBook) Subjects: LCSH: South Africa—Juvenile literature. | South Africa—Social life and customs—Juvenile literature. Classification: LCC DT1719 .P465 2016 | DDC 968—dc23 LC record available at http://lccn.loc.gov/2016008603

GLOSSARY

Afrikaans: a language spoken in South Africa that is based on Dutch

Ancestor: a family member who lived a long time ago

Basin: a low area of land into which bodies of water flow

Coast: land that touches a large body of water

Descendant: someone related to a person or group of people who lived a long time ago

Election: an event in which people vote for their leaders

Grassland: a large area of land covered by grass and small plants

Homelands: poor, crowded areas where many nonwhite South Africans were forced to live during apartheid

Northern Sotho: a language spoken in South Africa that is part of the Bantu language family

Plateau: a flat area of land that is raised higher than the land around it

Protest: an action or statement made by a person to show that he or she disagrees with something

Resist: to fight against or refuse to accept something

Rugby: a popular sport in South Africa that is similar to American football

Tribe: a group of people who share the same language and culture

Xhosa: a people who live mainly in South Africa; also a language spoken in South Africa that is part of the Bantu language family

Zulu: a people who live mainly in South Africa; also the most widely spoken language in South Africa; the language is part of the Bantu language family

NOTE TO READERS: Some of these words may have more than one definition. The definitions above are how these words are used in this book.

Dumela! (say: doo-MEL-ah) That means "hi" in Northern Sotho (say: SOO-too). My name is David, and I live in South Africa. South Africa is a country in Africa where more than fifty million people live . . . including me!

South Africa is on the
southern tip of Africa.
It borders six countries.
One of those countries,
Lesotho (say: leh-SOO-too),
is within South Africa's borders!

Much of South Africa is covered
by plateaus (say: pla-TOES),
which are tall, flat areas of land.
The plateaus have grasslands
on top.
Lots of animals, like rhinos,
zebras, cheetahs, lions, and
elephants live in the grasslands.

Above the plateaus, the land
dips down to form the
Kalahari (say: kah-lah-HAH-ree)
Basin. Some parts of the basin
are a sandy desert,
while other parts are grassy.

Along the coast is the Great Escarpment, where the plateaus drop off. Drakensberg is a very tall mountain range along the eastern part of the Great Escarpment. In the Afrikaans language, Drakensberg means "mountains of dragons"!

A very famous South African,
Archbishop Desmond Tutu, called
South Africa the "rainbow nation."
That's because South Africans come
from many different cultures.
Lots of people are descendants
of African tribes like the
Xhosa (say: K-OH-sah) and Zulu.

Some people trace their origins
to India. Their ancestors came to
South Africa as slaves or laborers
hundreds of years ago. Others are
descendants of Europeans
who came from Holland, France,
and England. Whatever our heritage,
today we are all South Africans.

JOHANNESBURG

South Africa has many big cities. Johannesburg was founded during a gold rush. A theme park was later built around one of the gold mines! Cape Town sits in the shadow of Table Mountain, a flat-topped mountain that looks down on the city.

CAPE TOWN

Bloemfontein (say: BLOOM-fohn-tane) is known as the city of roses. Its name means "fountain of flowers" in Dutch! Pretoria is home to the biggest zoo in South Africa. It houses many of the coolest plants and animals in our country!

I live in a house in a suburb
of Pretoria with my mom,
dad, older sister, and
older brother.

My dad is a software engineer.
He creates programs for computers.
My mom is an accountant.
She helps people with their money.
My sister wants to be a doctor
when she grows up. My brother
plays a sport called rugby.

We get up really early each
morning—around five thirty!
After I get dressed in my
school uniform, I have
breakfast with my family.
We usually eat cereal or
porridge.

Because my brother, sister,
and I go to a private school
in the city, we have a long
bus trip. We take our first
bus to downtown Pretoria
and our second bus to another
neighborhood where our school is.
The trip takes a little over an hour.

School starts at 7:45 a.m. There are thirty students in my class. Each day is split into eight different sections, or periods. We learn languages, math, science, music, gym, geography, and history. Our first lesson is history.

We have been learning about apartheid (say: ah-PAR-tate). Apartheid was a time in our history when the government discriminated against people of color. It began in 1948, when a group called the National Party won the election.

The National Party believed
that white people were better
than people of other races.
They forced anyone who wasn't
white to carry papers if
they wanted to travel outside
certain areas. Anyone caught
without their papers was arrested.

As time went on, things only
got worse. More than three million
people were forced to give up
their homes and land to the
government, which then resold
the land to white people. People
of other races were forced into poor,
crowded areas called "homelands."

People of other races who lived outside the homelands were separated from white South Africans in schools, theaters, and restaurants. On top of everything, the government stripped nonwhite people of their right to vote.

Many South Africans resisted apartheid, joining groups such as the African National Congress (ANC). Among the ANC's leaders was a lawyer named Nelson Mandela. Mandela organized protests and told people to fight apartheid laws. He was arrested for his beliefs.

Even though he was in jail, Mandela became a symbol for the resistance. By 1989, protests and demands from the people, as well as pressure from countries around the world, started to bring apartheid to an end. Nelson Mandela was released from prison in 1990.

In 1994, South Africans of
every race were able to vote
in the new elections.
Nelson Mandela won the
election to become South Africa's
first black president!

After our history lesson, we have languages. We learn English and Northern Sotho, but South Africa has eleven official languages in all! Some of the other official languages include Xhosa, Zulu, and Afrikaans.

After English, we work on our math lesson and then head to lunch. I usually pack a lunch from home, but today is Wednesday. That means it's macaroni and cheese day! I always eat a school lunch on Wednesdays.

After lunch we have lessons in geography and then science. In science we are learning about archaeology (say: ark-ay-AHL-oh-jee), or the study of how people in the past lived. There are many fossils and ancient cave paintings to study in South Africa!

Next we have music and gym class, and then school is over. My brother, sister, and I meet to walk to the bus stop. Once we get home, my sister helps me with my homework. Then I play a computer game.

When my parents get home, we go outside to play rugby. Rugby is a sport similar to American football. My brother and I have played rugby in summer programs. Rugby is one of the most popular sports in South Africa.